Let's Go to A HoneyFarm Bee

Series- *Children's Knowledge Quest*

Author

M Borhan

From

Big 6 Publishing

Pencil Sketch of a Farm Hive from 19th Century

Honey
Bee Farm
Honey cultivation, also known as beekeeping or
Apiculture, involves managing honey bee colonies
to extract honey and other hive products.

Setting Up the Apiary
Beekeepers start by setting up an apiary, which is a location where beehives are kept.

Location of Apiary
The location should have access to nectar and pollen sources, such as flowering plants and trees.

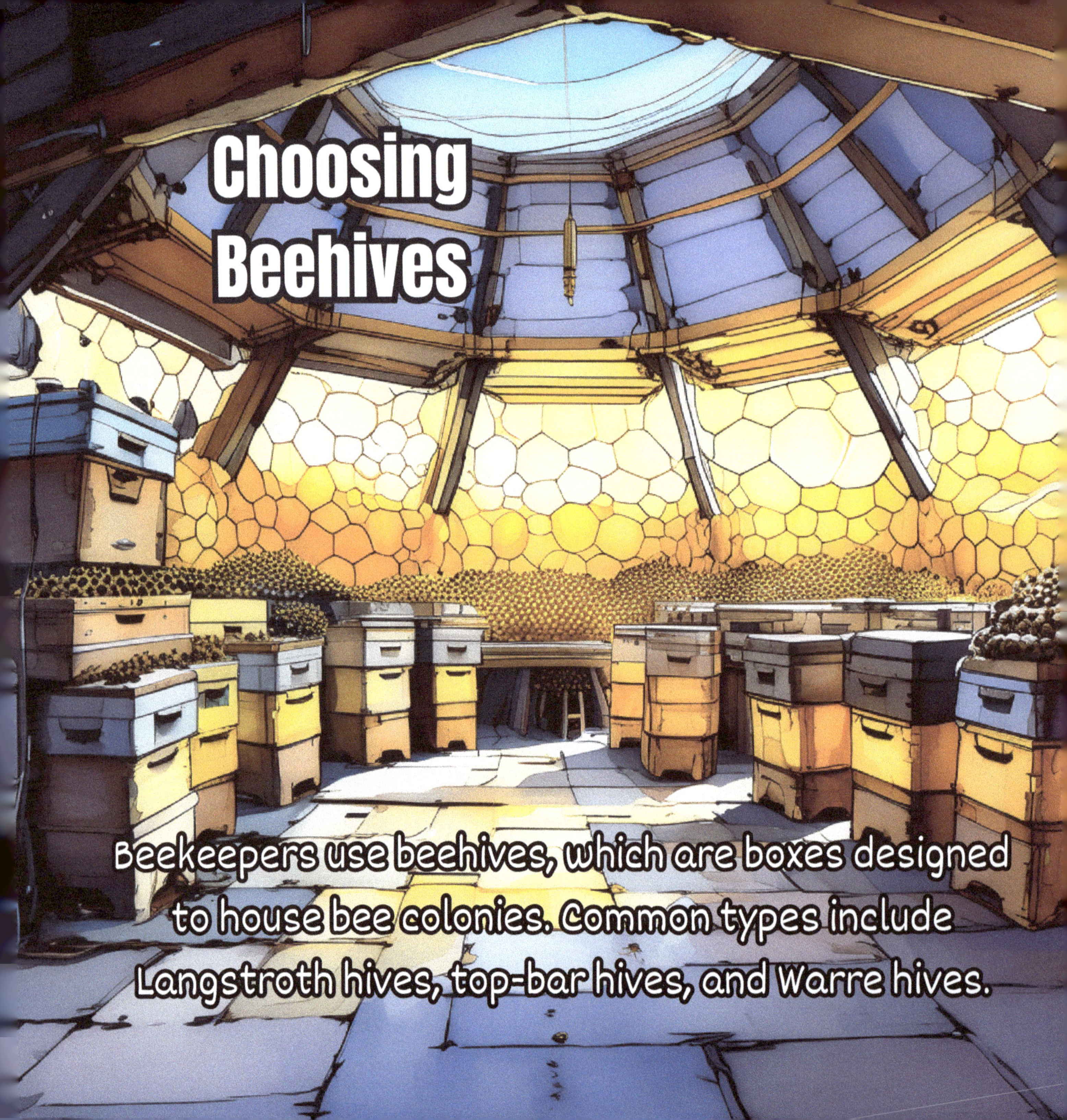

Choosing Beehives
Beekeepers use beehives, which are boxes designed to house bee colonies. Common types include Langstroth hives, top-bar hives, and Warre hives.

Structure
of the Hives
The beehives consist of boxes with removable frames that contain comb for bees to build their colonies.

Different Types of Bee-Hives
Beehives, like Langstroth hives, house colonies are popularly used, these provide homes for honey bee colonies.. Other hive types, like top-bar and Warre, may be used.

Introducing Bees to Hives
Beekeepers introduce bees to the hives. This can be done by purchasing packaged bees and then giving them their hives open to enter.

Bee Swarm Cultivation
This process can be done by capturing a swarm and then make them abound in the definite bee-hive or bee-structure made for them.

Members of the Colony
The queen bee, worker bees, and drones are essential components of a healthy colony.

Colony
Management
Beekeepers regularly inspect their colonies to ensure the health and productivity of the bees.

Population
Monitoring
They may monitor the population, check for signs
of disease, and assess the availability of food
sources.

Nectar Collection
Honey bees collect nectar from flowering plants using their proboscis.

Nectar Processing
Microscopic Ultra High Definition View
Nectar is a sugary liquid produced by flowers, and bees store it in a specialized stomach called the honey crop.

Honey Production
Microscopic Ultra High Definition View
Bees convert the collected nectar into honey through a process of regurgitation and evaporation.

Honey Deposit
They deposit the nectar in the hive cells, and worker bees fan their wings to speed up the drying process.

Comb Building
Alongside these,
Bees build comb from beeswax to store honey,
pollen, and raise brood (developing bees).

Hive Products

Harvesting Honey
Beekeepers harvest honey when the bees have capped the cells, indicating that the honey is ready for storage.

Extracting Honey

Harvesting typically involves removing frames with capped honey and extracting the honey using a centrifugal extractor.

Processing Honey

Bottling Honey
The processed honey is then bottled for sale or personal use.

Caring for Bees in Winter
In colder climates, beekeepers take steps to ensure their colonies survive the winter, they are given warm sunlighting environment places.

Supplementary Elements for the Winter

This may involve providing supplemental food, insulating hives, and managing pests. Finally, the bees find thier supplementary environment.

At the End
of the Winter
After the Winter, the Bee Hive Frames & Boxes are
brought outside for some time to match the weather
environment nature and then brought in again...
Thus starts a new year for Honey...